Funny Scenarios

For kids and adults

Would you rather?

Funny Scenarios

ISBN-10: 1790932297
ISBN-13: 978-1790932290

Printed in the United States of America

CONTENTS

Would you rather:

...be personal friends with Batman

-or-

enemy with Joker?

Would you rather:

...kiss a jellyfish

-or-

step on a hedgehog?

Would you rather:

...meet your favorite superhero

-or-

the President of the United States?

Would you rather:

...speak all languages

-or-

be able to speak to all animals?

Would you rather:

...kiss Justin Timberlake

-or-

Woody Woodpeker?

Would you rather:

...eat a whole turkey

-or-

never eat turkey again?

Would you rather:

...watch "Home Alone"

-or-

sing "Get along little doggies, get along"?

Would you rather:

... have a big cookie

-or-

a small magic cake?

Would you rather:

...travel back in time to a last winter holiday

-or-

travel to a future one?

Would you rather:

...ride in a one horse open sleigh

-or-

go walking in a winter wonderland?

Would you rather:

…decorate cookies

-or-

a gingerbread house?

Would you rather:

…experience an epic waterslide

-or-

an epic zip line?

Would you rather:

...live in a tree house

-or-

a castle?

Would you rather:

...hang 10 strands of tinsel one at a time

-or-

100 ornaments?

Would you rather:

...not celebrate Christmas

-or-

not celebrate Helloween?

Would you rather:

...live in a house made of gummy bears

-or-

marshmallows?

Would you rather:

...be the best singer

-or-

the best dancer in your school?

Would you rather:

...spend the holidays with your family

with super heroes?

Would you rather:

...drink hot chocolate in the summer

-or-

eat ice cream in the winter.

Would you rather:

...lose all your Christmas presents

-or-

lose your Christmas memories?

Would you rather:

…clean the reindeer barn

-or-

the elf workshop?

Would you rather:

…eat gum that is already chewed

-or-

a candy cane that has been licked?

Would you rather:

...cook the holiday meal

-or-

wash the dishes after the holiday meal?

Would you rather:

...go to school on holiday

-or-

never go to school again?

Would you rather:

...give up Christmas tree

-or-

Christmas cookies?

Would you rather:

...have Thanksgiving at Disneyland

-or-

with your family?

Would you rather:

...have to eat only Christmas food

-or-

watch only Christmas movies?

Would you rather:

...have head like pumpkin

-or-

eat a huge pumpkin pie?

Would you rather:

…have to wear your shoes on the wrong feet

-or-

your pants backwards?

Would you rather:

…have to brush your teeth with a dirty toothbrush

-or-

wipe your butt with dirty toilet paper?

Would you rather:

...take a trip down the Amazon River

-or-

walk by the Great Wall of China?

Would you rather:

...eat popsicles

-or-

watermelon?

Would you rather:

...rock around Christmas tree

-or-

fight with dinosaurs in the jungle?

Would you rather:

...eat soap

-or-

get your tongue stuck to a pole?

Would you rather:

...be Mister Heat Miser

-or-

Mister Freeze?

Would you rather:

...be able to talk to frogs

-or-

talk to snakes?

Would you rather:

...get yelled at by your mom

-or-

your teacher?

Would you rather:

...have elf ears

-or-

a Santa's beard?

Would you rather:

...never get sick

-or-

never go to school again?

Would you rather:

...be bald

-or-

have hair everywhere?

Would you rather:

…have 6 geese a laying

-or-

7 swans a swimming?

Would you rather:

…make toy trains

-or-

crying dolls?

Would you rather:

...have a dinosaur friend

~or~

be a dinosaur?

Would you rather:

...be able to sing like Lady Gaga

-or-

be able to move like Jagger?

Would you rather:

...sing Jingle Bells nonstop for 1 hour

-or-

sing 20 different carols without a break?

Would you rather:

...be a class president

-or-

a homecoming king / queen?

Would you rather:

...ride on the back of an elephant

-or-

a hippo?

Would you rather:

...have overly large hands

-or-

very small feet?

Would you rather:

...find true love

-or-

find one million dollars?

Would you rather:

...be able to talk with animals

-or-

be able to speak all foreign languages?

Would you rather:

...give up pizza

-or-

turkey?

Would you rather:

...take a bath in a milkshake

-or-

chocolate pudding?

Would you rather:

...wash your hair with cranberry sauce

-or-

put a turkey on your head?

Would you rather:

...always know when someone is lying

-or-

let some stuff stay secret?

Would you rather:

...be able to control your dreams

-or-

be able to watch your dreams on video?

Would you rather:

...go left where nothing is right

-or-

right where nothing is left?

Would you rather:

... read an awesome book

-or-

watch a movie?

Would you rather:

…have an evil dog as a pet

-or-

a silly cat as a pet?

Would you rather:

...have Christmas decorations all year

-or-

never have them again?

Would you rather:

...eat pumpkin pie every day

-or-

eat candy canes every day?

Would you rather:

...be a kid your whole life

-or-

an adult your whole life?

Would you rather:

...be able to create a new holiday

-or-

create a new sport?

Would you rather:

...be a reindeer

-or-

a ghost?

Would you rather:

...be a Secret Santa for your best friend

-or-

your best friend be Secret Santa to you?

Would you rather:

...get stuck in a supermarket during Christmas

-or-

at the airport?

Would you rather:

...be able to play the piano

-or-

the guitar?

Would you rather:

...live forever

-or-

have all candy in the world?

Would you rather:

...receive one huge present for Christmas

-or-

a hundred small ones?

Would you rather:

...be a movie star

-or-

singer?

Would you rather:

...lick a frog

-or-

eat a maggot?

Would you rather:

...visit Hogwarts

-or-

meet Jon Snow?

Would you rather:

...live without music

-or-

without internet?

Would you rather:

...pull Santa's sleigh

-or-

lift pumpkins?

Would you rather:

...be a doctor

-or-

a garbage man?

Would you rather:

...have to sit all day

-or-

stand all night?

Would you rather:

...be invisible during holidays

-or-

fly during holiday?

Would you rather:

...be a turkey farmer

-or-

a pumpkin farmer?

Would you rather:

…have more friends

-or-

more presents?

Would you rather:

...smell your own fart

-or-

smell someone else's?

Would you rather:

...never play basketball

-or-

play but always lose?

Would you rather:

...be Santa

-or-

a superhero?

Would you rather:

...have hiccups for a long time

-or-

feel itchy for the rest of your life?

Would you rather:

...eat dog food

-or-

a rotten apple?

Would you rather:

...be a parent

-or-

a child?

Would you rather:

...have super strong fingers

-or-

super fast lips?

Would you rather:

...dance all year

-or-

step by step draw all Christmas?

Would you rather:

...wear winter clothes in summer

-or-

summer clothes in winter?

Would you rather:

...have a unicorn horn

-or-

a reindeer nose?

Would you rather:

...live in the desert

-or-

in the jungle?

Would you rather:

...drink a glass of liquid soap

-or-

a glass of vinegar?

Would you rather:

...fart in front of your friends

-or-

pee in your pants in front of them?

Would you rather:

...lose your ears

-or-

your tongue?

Would you rather:

...eat a whole onion

-or-

a lemon?

Would you rather:

...have green hair

-or-

purple eyes?

Would you rather:

...get a trick

-or-

a treat?

Would you rather:

...meet an alien

-or-

lose your favorite toy?

Would you rather:

...eat bread with black butter

-or-

drink tea with sand?

Would you rather:

...live in a spaceship

-or-

in a castle?

Would you rather:

...have a twin

-or-

be an only child?

Would you rather:

...never be able to shout

-or-

never be able to whisper?

Would you rather:

...get lots of kiss and hugs

-or-

lots of kicks?

Would you rather:

...swim in a river full of snakes

-or-

lay on bed full of spiders?

Would you rather:

...have a pet dinosaur from Jurassic Park

-or-

a pet dragon?

Would you rather:

...not be able to see green color

-or-

taste sweets?

Would you rather:

...meet an Easter bunny

-or-

find lots of Easter eggs?

Would you rather:

...walk on water

-or-

fly under earth?

Would you rather:

...be in a food fight

-or-

just watch a food fight?

Would you rather:

...have a hundred of friends

-or-

a robot friend?

Would you rather:

...lick milk like a cat

-or-

lick yourself like a cat?

Would you rather:

...be Frosty the snowman

-or-

Rudolf, the Red-Nosed Reindeer?

Would you rather:

...be personal friends with Batman

-or-

enemy with Spiderman?

Would you rather:

...kiss a jellyfish

-or-

step on a hedgehog?

Would you rather:

...five years older

-or-

five years younger?

Would you rather:

...get to eat whatever you want, whenever you want

-or-

get to go to bed whenever you want?

Would you rather:

...spend Christmas in the city

-or-

in the country?

Would you rather:

...be one of Santa's reindeer

-or-

one of his elves?

Would you rather:

...be a rockstar

-or-

a famous actor when you grow up?

Would you rather:

...win an Olympic gold medal

-or-

win a million dollar in the lottery?

Would you rather:

...stay in a gingerbread house

-or-

travel on the Polar Express?

Would you rather:

...spend a night in a haunted house

-or-

never celebrate Halloween again?

Would you rather:

...have the power to run as fast as the speed of light

-or-

the power to walk through walls?

Would you rather:

...be great at math

-or-

great at English?

Would you rather:

...ride a horse

-or-

a camel?

Would you rather:

....meet a fairy

-or-

a unicorn?!!!

Would you rather:

...have a huge bounce house

-or-

a huge ball pit in your backyard?

Would you rather:

...travel to the Sahara Desert

-or-

travel to the Moon and back?

Would you rather:

...have a swimming pool

-or-

the coolest treehouse in your backyard?

Would you rather:

...get to eat pizza

-or-

hamburgers for dinner every night?

Would you rather:

...have a scary smile

-or-

have a really loud laugh?

Would you rather:

...look like old man

-or-

look like a newborn baby again?

Would you rather:

...fart really loud

-or-

poop your pants silently?

Would you rather:

...have free tickets wherever you go

-or-

have free candy whenever you want?

Would you rather:

...have a monkey instead of brother

-or-

a pet tiger?

Would you rather:

...be captain of the football team

-or-

captain of the monster team?

Would you rather:

...be able to see in the dark

-or-

be able to never get tired?

Would you rather:

...eat an entire cake

-or-

an entire carton of ice cream?

Would you rather:

...be the best looking person in your class

-or-

the smartest?

Would you rather:

...be able to fly

-or-

be able to breathe underwater?

Would you rather:

...have a shiny nose

-or-

two eyes made out of coal?

Would you rather:

...be able to sing beautifully

-or-

dance ugly?

Would you rather:

...know where you're going

-or-

have it be a surprise?

Would you rather:

...swim in the ocean

-or-

swim in a pool?

Would you rather:

...be a dolphin

-or-

a cheetah?

Would you rather:

...be able to make people laugh

-or-

be able to make people trust you?

Would you rather:

...be surprised by a present

-or-

be able to pick what you get?

Would you rather:

...be the ghost of Christmas past

-or-

the ghost of Christmas present?

Would you rather:

...get the present you have always wanted

-or-

ride in the sleigh with Santa?

Would you rather:

...make a snowman

-or-

have a snowball fight?

Funny Scenarios

Holiday Jokes

***

- Knock, knock.

- Who's there?

- M. C. and H. N. Y.

- M. C. who?

- Merry Christmas and Happy New Year!

***

- Knock, knock.

- Who's there?

- Hope.

- Hope who?

- Hope you had a nice holiday!

Funny Scenarios

***

– Knock, knock.

– Who's there?

– Donut.

– Donut who?

– Donut open till Christmas!

***

– Knock, knock.

– Who's there?

– Snow.

– Snow who?

– Snowbody!

Funny Scenarios

***

Q: What did Adam say the day before Christmas?

A: It's Christmas, Eve!

***

Q: What does a snowman eat for breakfast?

A: Snowflakes.

***

Q: What is Tarzan's favourite Christmas carol?

A: Jungle Bells.

***

Q: Who is Santa's favorite singer?

A: Elf-is Presley!

LEAVE A REVIEW PLEASE!

If you have enjoyed this book, please consider leaving a short review on the books Amazon page. It will help the others to make an informed decision before buying my book.

Thank you so much.

Funny Scenarios

Made in the USA
Middletown, DE
19 February 2019